STIR-FRY

CHOPWOKTOSSCHOPWOKTOSSCHOPWOKTOSS

THE AUSTRALIAN Women's Weekly

CONTENTS

My wok is used as much as my saucepans these days; stir-fries are the ultimate fast food – they're not only quick to make, but also easy and fairly low in fat. As you browse through this book, you'll discover that stir-fries aren't necessarily Asian; no matter what cuisine you crave, there's a stir-fry to fit your wok.

Pamela Clark

Food Director

WOK BASICS

Before you start stir-frying, make sure your wok is prepared

Our obsession with Asian cooking (which is not only delicious but easy to prepare and healthy), means that it is now commonplace to see stir-fries on our dinner tables a few times a week and a wok in the cupboard next to our saucepans and casserole dishes.

However, before you start stir-frying, you need to prepare your equipment. A stir-fry is best done in a wok – the shape makes tossing ingredients together easy. Choose your wok carefully. They are available in most department stores, Asian cooking stores and homewares stores. A round-based wok is more traditional, and works well on gas burners, while a wok with a flat base is better on electric stoves.

SEASONING YOUR WOK

Before use, a wok must be seasoned if it is made from cast-iron or carbon steel. (Stainless steel and non-stick woks do not need seasoning.) Seasoning is a way of "ageing" the wok primarily so that food does not stick to the surface when being cooked; this also facilitates washing up. Seasoning also helps enhance flavours during cooking.

To season a wok, wash the wok in hot soapy water to remove all traces of grease and lacquer (woks are sometimes coated with a thin film of lacquer to prevent rusting during shipping). Dry the wok thoroughly. Place the wok on the stove over high heat. If you're worried about setting off your smoke alarm or filling the kitchen with smoke, you may prefer to season the wok outside on the barbecue. When the

wok is hot, rub 1 to 2 tablespoons of peanut oil, which has a high smoke point that can handle high heat without burning, over the entire inside surface with absorbent paper. Wear oven gloves on both hands for this step as both the oil and the wok become very hot. Continue heating the wok for 10-15 minutes, wiping from time to time with a ball of clean absorbent paper. This will create a certain amount of smoke and is perfectly normal because you are effectively "burning off" the oil on the surface of the wok.

Allow the wok to cool completely then repeat the heating and wiping process twice more (a total of three times). Your wok is now ready to use.

To wash the wok after cooking, use warm soapy water (never use abrasives or scourers) and dry it well.

PREPARE YOUR INGREDIENTS

Because stir-frying a dish only takes a matter of minutes, it's important to be prepared in advance. Meat and vegetables should be cut to a uniform size and thickness to ensure even cooking, and stocks, sauces and liquids should be measured and ready to add.

Meat should be cooked first, in batches, so that the food sizzles as it cooks. If there's too much food in the wok, the food will "stew" rather than fry, making it tough and unpalatable. Cook vegetables of the hardest texture first, then add leafy vegetables towards the end to ensure your stir-fries are full of colour and look spectacular.

FAST

Meat, vegetables, wok. What could be simpler?

peanut chilli beef with choy sum

PREPARATION TIME **10 MINUTES**   COOKING TIME **15 MINUTES**   SERVES **4**

700g beef strips
½ cup (140g) crunchy peanut butter
¼ cup (75g) sambal oelek
¼ cup (60ml) kecap manis
2 tablespoons peanut oil
2 medium white onions (300g), cut into 8 wedges
½ small wombok (350g), shredded coarsely
400g choy sum, chopped coarsely

1   Place beef in medium bowl with half the peanut butter, 2 teaspoons of the sambal and 2 teaspoons of the kecap manis; rub peanut butter mixture into beef.
2   Combine remaining peanut butter, sambal and kecap manis in small jug.
3   Heat half the oil in wok; stir-fry beef, in batches, until cooked as desired. Cover to keep warm.
4   Heat remaining oil in wok; stir-fry onion and wombok, in batches, until browned lightly. Return onion and wombok to wok with choy sum; stir-fry to combine, then pour reserved peanut butter mixture into wok. Stir-fry until choy sum just wilts and mixture is hot.
5   Serve vegetable mixture topped with beef.
per serving 37.7g total fat (9g saturated fat); 2541kJ (608 cal); 13.8g carbohydrate; 50.7g protein; 7.2g fibre

peking duck in a wok

PREPARATION TIME **10 MINUTES** COOKING TIME **10 MINUTES** SERVES **4**

1 chinese barbecued duck (1kg)
24 peking duck pancakes (240g)
4 green onions, cut into thin strips
⅔ cup (160ml) hoisin sauce
2 cups (160g) bean sprouts
2 lebanese cucumbers (260g), halved lengthways, seeded, cut into thin strips

Buy a barbecued duck and a packet of peking duck pancakes at an Asian food shop on your way home from work and you'll have a great dinner on the table in a few minutes – so easy and so delicious.

1   Remove meat and skin from duck; discard bones. Chop meat and skin coarsely.
2   Heat pancakes by folding each into quarters, place in steamer set over large pan of simmering water; steam until warm and pliable.
3   Heat wok; stir-fry duck and onion until onion just softens. Add half the sauce; stir-fry until hot.
4   Remove from heat; stir in sprouts. Serve duck mixture with pancakes, cucumber and remaining sauce.
per serving 40.6g total fat (11.6g saturated fat); 2713kJ (649 cal); 35.1g carbohydrate; 33.5g protein; 7.3g fibre

barbecued pork with hokkien noodles

PREPARATION TIME **10 MINUTES** COOKING TIME **10 MINUTES** SERVES **4**

1 tablespoon peanut oil
4 green onions, chopped coarsely
2 cloves garlic, sliced thinly
1 medium red capsicum (200g),
  sliced thinly
½ cup (190g) char siu sauce
2 tablespoons sambal oelek

¼ cup (60ml) water
2 tablespoons lime juice
4cm piece fresh ginger (20g), grated
1 cup (120g) frozen peas
400g chinese barbecued pork,
  sliced thinly
440g fresh thin hokkien noodles

1   Heat oil in wok; stir-fry onion, garlic and capsicum 1 minute.
2   Add remaining ingredients; stir-fry until peas are just cooked and mixture is hot.
per serving 7.4g total fat (1.2g saturated fat); 719kJ (172 cal); 22.3g carbohydrate; 1.9g protein; 5.9g fibre

hoisin sweet chilli lamb and mixed vegetables

PREPARATION TIME **10 MINUTES** COOKING TIME **15 MINUTES** SERVES **4**

1 tablespoon peanut oil
750g lamb strips
2 cloves garlic, sliced thinly
400g packaged fresh stir-fry vegetables
⅓ cup (80ml) hoisin sauce
2 tablespoons sweet chilli sauce
2 tablespoons water

1   Heat half the oil in wok; stir-fry lamb, in batches, until cooked.
2   Heat remaining oil in wok; stir-fry garlic and vegetables until vegetables are almost tender. Return lamb to wok with sauces and the water; stir-fry until hot.
per serving 23.1g total fat (8.7g saturated fat); 1877kJ (449 cal); 17.2g carbohydrate; 41.4g protein; 4.5g fibre

singapore curry noodles

PREPARATION TIME **10 MINUTES** COOKING TIME **10 MINUTES** SERVES **4**

1 small brown onion (80g), sliced thinly
2 bacon rashers (140g), chopped finely
2 teaspoons curry powder
3 cups (480g) shredded barbecued chicken
6 green onions, sliced thinly
2 tablespoons soy sauce
⅓ cup (80ml) sweet sherry
3cm piece fresh ginger (15g), grated
400g fresh thin rice noodles

You need to purchase a large barbecued chicken weighing approximately 900g to get the amount of shredded meat required for this recipe.

1   Heat wok; stir-fry brown onion and bacon until bacon is crisp. Add curry powder; stir-fry until fragrant.
2   Add chicken, green onion, sauce, sherry and ginger; stir-fry to combine. Add noodles; stir-fry, tossing gently, until hot.
per serving 12.9g total fat (4.1g saturated fat); 1517kJ (363 cal); 25.9g carbohydrate; 30.1g protein; 1.4g fibre

tamarind honey prawns with pineapple

PREPARATION TIME **20 MINUTES** COOKING TIME **15 MINUTES** SERVES **4**

1.2kg uncooked medium king prawns
1 tablespoon vegetable oil
3 cloves garlic, crushed
1 fresh long red chilli, sliced thinly
1 medium red capsicum (200g),
  sliced thinly
150g snow peas, trimmed

⅓ cup (100g) tamarind concentrate
2 tablespoons kecap manis
1 tablespoon honey
230g can bamboo shoots, rinsed, drained
½ small pineapple (450g),
  chopped coarsely
4 green onions, sliced thinly

1   Shell and devein prawns, leaving tails intact.
2   Heat oil in wok; stir-fry prawns, garlic, chilli, capsicum and peas until prawns
are changed in colour. Add remaining ingredients; stir-fry until hot.
per serving 5.8g total fat (0.8g saturated fat); 1141kJ (273 cal); 18.5g carbohydrate;
34.6g protein; 4.3g fibre

wasabi tuna with warm sesame noodles

PREPARATION TIME **10 MINUTES** COOKING TIME **15 MINUTES** SERVES **4**

600g tuna steaks, cut into 2cm pieces
2 tablespoons wasabi paste
1 tablespoon sesame oil
250g dried soba noodles
300g sugar snap peas

2 green onions, sliced thinly
2 tablespoons sesame seeds
1 tablespoon rice wine vinegar
2 tablespoons kecap asin

1   Combine fish in medium bowl with wasabi and half the oil; rub wasabi
mixture into fish.
2   Cook noodles in large saucepan of boiling water, uncovered, until just
tender; stir in peas and green onion, drain immediately. Place in large bowl.
3   Meanwhile, heat wok; roast sesame seeds until browned lightly. Add to
noodles with remaining oil, vinegar and kecap asin; toss to combine.
4   Stir-fry fish in hot wok until cooked (do not overcook or fish will dry out).
Serve noodles topped with fish.
per serving 20.7g total fat (5g saturated fat); 2462kJ (589 cal); 47.6g carbohydrate;
49.4g protein; 5.6g fibre

SEAFOOD

Stir-frying helps seafood retain its delicate taste and firm texture

chilli squid with mint and bean sprout salad

PREPARATION TIME **25 MINUTES** COOKING TIME **10 MINUTES** SERVES **4**

1kg squid hoods, cleaned
½ teaspoon cracked black pepper
⅓ cup fried shallots
½ teaspoon dried chilli flakes
2 teaspoons sea salt flakes
2 tablespoons vegetable oil

MINT AND BEAN SPROUT SALAD
½ cup (125ml) lime juice
1 tablespoon fish sauce
2 tablespoons grated palm sugar
1 cup coarsely chopped fresh mint
2½ cups (200g) bean sprouts
2 lebanese cucumbers (260g), seeded,
    sliced thinly
2 fresh long red chillies, sliced thinly

1 Cut squid down centre to open out; score inside in diagonal pattern
then cut into thick strips.
2 Using mortar and pestle, crush pepper, shallots, chilli and salt.
3 Make mint and bean sprout salad.
4 Heat oil in wok; stir-fry squid, in batches, until cooked through. Combine
squid in large bowl with spice mixture; serve with salad.
MINT AND BEAN SPROUT SALAD Combine juice, sauce and sugar in medium
bowl. Add remaining ingredients; toss salad gently to combine.
per serving 11.2g total fat (1.7g saturated fat); 978kJ (234 cal); 10g carbohydrate;
21.1g protein; 3.3g fibre

char kway teow

PREPARATION TIME **20 MINUTES** COOKING TIME **15 MINUTES** SERVES **4**

450g wide fresh rice noodles
250g uncooked small prawns
250g squid hoods
⅓ cup (80ml) peanut oil
250g firm white fish fillets, skinned,
  cut into 3cm pieces
2 cloves garlic, crushed
2 fresh small red thai chillies,
  chopped finely

4cm piece fresh ginger (20g), grated
2 eggs, beaten lightly
5 green onions, sliced thinly
2 cups (160g) bean sprouts
120g dried chinese sausage, sliced thinly
2 tablespoons dark soy sauce
1 tablespoon kecap manis
1 tablespoon light soy sauce

Dried chinese sausages, also called lop chong, are usually made from pork but can also be made with duck liver or beef. Red-brown in colour and sweet-spicy in flavour, the 12cm dried links are sold, several strung together, in all Asian food stores.

1 Place noodles in large heatproof bowl; cover with boiling water, separate with fork, drain.
2 Shell and devein prawns, leaving tails intact. Cut squid down centre to open out; score inside in diagonal pattern, then cut into 2cm-wide strips.
3 Heat 1 tablespoon of the oil in wok; stir-fry fish and squid, in batches, until browned lightly. Place in large bowl; cover to keep warm.
4 Heat another tablespoon of the oil in wok; stir-fry prawns, garlic, chilli and ginger until prawns just change colour. Add to bowl with fish and squid; cover to keep warm.
5 Heat remaining oil in wok; stir-fry egg, onion and sprouts until egg is just set. Slide egg mixture onto plate; cover to keep warm.
6 Stir-fry sausage in wok until crisp; drain. Return sausage to wok with seafood, egg mixture, sauces and noodles; stir-fry until hot.
per serving 29.9g total fat (6.9g saturated fat); 2291kJ (548 cal); 27g carbohydrate; 41.1g protein; 3.3g fibre

garlic prawns

PREPARATION TIME **15 MINUTES** COOKING TIME **10 MINUTES** SERVES **4**

24 uncooked medium prawns (1kg)
60g butter
2 tablespoons vegetable oil
5 cloves garlic, chopped finely
2 fresh small red thai chillies,
  chopped finely
1 small red onion (100g), sliced thinly

4 medium egg tomatoes (300g),
  chopped coarsely
½ cup coarsely chopped fresh
  flat-leaf parsley
2 tablespoons balsamic vinegar
1 large loaf sourdough bread (675g),
  sliced thickly

1   Shell and devein prawns, leaving tails intact.
2   Heat butter and oil in wok; cook garlic, chilli and onion, stirring, until onion softens. Add prawns, in batches; stir-fry until changed in colour and cooked through.
3   Remove from heat, stir in tomato and parsley, drizzle with vinegar; serve prawns with bread.
per serving 26.9g total fat (10.1g saturated fat); 3131kJ (749 cal); 79.4g carbohydrate; 41.7g protein; 10.2g fibre

mussels with kaffir lime and thai basil

PREPARATION TIME **30 MINUTES** COOKING TIME **10 MINUTES** SERVES **4**

1.5kg small black mussels
1 tablespoon peanut oil
3cm piece fresh ginger (15g), sliced thinly
1 clove garlic, sliced thinly
2 shallots (50g), sliced thinly
2 fresh long red chillies, sliced thinly
½ teaspoon ground turmeric
¼ cup (60ml) kecap manis

¼ cup (60ml) fish stock
¼ cup (60ml) water
2 tablespoons lime juice
2 fresh kaffir lime leaves, shredded finely
½ cup firmly packed fresh
  coriander leaves
½ cup firmly packed thai basil leaves

1   Scrub mussels under cold water; remove beards.
2   Heat oil in wok; stir-fry ginger, garlic, shallot, chilli and turmeric until fragrant. Add kecap manis, stock and the water; bring to a boil. Add mussels; simmer, covered, about 5 minutes or until mussels open (discard any that do not).
3   Remove from heat; add remaining ingredients; toss gently to combine.
per serving 5.6g total fat (1.1g saturated fat); 414kJ (99 cal); 3.9g carbohydrate; 7.5g protein; 0.7g fibre

SHORT-ORDER

prawn salad A fresh prawn salad is just the thing for hot summer evenings. Shell and devein the prawns, stir-fry them with a little vegetable oil, chopped onion and crushed garlic until prawns are just changed in colour. Serve with some coarsely chopped tomato, fresh sliced chilli, fresh parsley leaves and large lettuce leaves (such as butter lettuce). Dress with balsamic vinegar and you'll have a mouth-watering starter or light lunch.

five-spice and chilli fish with blood orange

PREPARATION TIME **20 MINUTES (PLUS REFRIGERATION TIME)** COOKING TIME **15 MINUTES** SERVES **4**

¼ cup (60ml) light soy sauce
2 teaspoons five-spice powder
2 cloves garlic, crushed
1 fresh long red chilli, sliced thinly
1 teaspoon finely grated blood
  orange rind
5 baby onions (125g), sliced thinly

800g blue-eye fillets, cut into 2cm pieces
2 tablespoons peanut oil
350g broccolini, trimmed,
  chopped coarsely
2 tablespoons water
4 green onions, sliced thickly
4 small blood oranges (720g), segmented

We used blue-eye in our recipe, but you can use any firm white fish fillets.

1   Combine 2 tablespoons of the sauce in medium bowl with five-spice, garlic, chilli, rind and baby onion; add fish, turn to coat in mixture. Cover; refrigerate 1 hour.
2   Heat half the oil in wok; stir-fry fish mixture, in batches, until cooked as desired.
3   Heat remaining oil in wok; stir-fry broccolini with the water and remaining sauce until tender.
4   Return fish mixture to wok with green onion and orange, stir-fry until hot.
per serving 11g total fat (1.9g saturated fat); 1409kJ (337 cal); 13.4g carbohydrate; 41.9g protein; 7.1g fibre

chicken, peanuts and lots of chillies. An authentic Sichuan-Chinese restaurant always has a delicious kung pao.

choy sum; stir-fry until wilted. Return prawns to wok with sauce, wine, sugar and chestnuts; stir-fry 2 minutes. Remove from heat; stir in onion and nuts.
per serving 19.4g total fat (2.9g saturated fat); 1998kJ (478 cal); 8.5g carbohydrate; 8.5g protein; 7.5g fibre

orange-flavoured octopus and broccolini

PREPARATION TIME **20 MINUTES (PLUS REFRIGERATION TIME)** COOKING TIME **15 MINUTES** SERVES **4**

½ cup (150g) tamarind concentrate
¼ cup (60ml) japanese soy sauce
1 teaspoon finely grated orange rind
⅓ cup (80ml) orange juice
1 tablespoon honey
½ teaspoon ground cumin
2 cloves garlic, crushed
2cm piece fresh ginger (10g), grated
1 fresh long red chilli, chopped finely

⅓ cup (80ml) peanut oil
1kg whole cleaned baby
  octopus, quartered
1 medium brown onion (150g),
  sliced thinly
350g broccolini, chopped coarsely
200g snow peas
¼ cup (40g) roasted unsalted cashews
1 fresh long red chilli, sliced thinly

1   Combine tamarind, sauce, rind, juice, honey, cumin, garlic, ginger, chopped chilli
and half the oil in large bowl; add octopus, mix well. Cover; refrigerate 1 hour.
2   Drain octopus over medium bowl; reserve ½ cup marinade.
3   Heat half the remaining oil in wok; stir-fry octopus, in batches, until tender.
4   Heat remaining oil in cleaned wok; stir-fry onion until soft. Add broccolini and
snow peas; stir-fry until tender.
5   Return octopus to wok with reserved marinade; bring to a boil then remove from
heat (do not overcook or octopus will toughen). Stir in nuts, sprinkle with sliced chilli.
*per serving 28.1g total fat (5.2g saturated fat); 2688kJ (643 cal); 21.7g carbohydrate;
72.9g protein; 6.9g fibre*

POULTRY

Stir-frying brings out the tenderness and simple flavours of poultry

chengdu chicken

PREPARATION TIME **20 MINUTES (PLUS REFRIGERATION TIME)** COOKING TIME **15 MINUTES** SERVES **4**

2 tablespoons light soy sauce
2 tablespoons chinese cooking wine
1 teaspoon sesame oil
800g chicken breast fillets,
  chopped coarsely
¼ cup (60ml) peanut oil
300g spinach, trimmed,
  chopped coarsely

2 cloves garlic, crushed
2cm piece fresh ginger (10g), grated
4 green onions, sliced thinly
1 tablespoon rice vinegar
1 teaspoon white sugar
2 tablespoons finely grated orange rind
2 tablespoons sambal oelek
1 teaspoon sichuan peppercorns, crushed

Sichuan cuisine, also known as Szechuan-style, is one of the most popular regional styles of Chinese cooking and is characterised by its spicy and pungent flavours. An ingredient often used is citrus peel; its inclusion offers proof that the dish is native to Chengdu, the capital of Sichuan.

1 Combine half the sauce, half the wine and half the sesame oil in large bowl; add chicken, mix well. Cover; refrigerate 20 minutes.
2 Heat 1 tablespoon of the peanut oil in wok; stir-fry spinach until just wilted. Remove from wok; cover to keep warm.
3 Heat half the remaining peanut oil in wok; stir-fry chicken mixture, in batches, until browned. Heat remaining peanut oil in wok; stir-fry garlic, ginger and onion until onion just softens.
4 Return chicken and remaining sauce, wine and sesame oil to wok with vinegar, sugar, rind and sambal; stir-fry until chicken is cooked.
5 Serve spinach topped with chicken; sprinkle with pepper.
per serving 19.8g total fat (3.8g saturated fat); 1710kJ (409 cal); 5.7g carbohydrate; 48g protein; 2.1g fibre

capsicum, chilli and hoisin chicken

PREPARATION TIME **15 MINUTES (PLUS REFRIGERATION TIME)** COOKING TIME **15 MINUTES** SERVES **4**

800g chicken breast fillets, sliced thinly
2 cloves garlic, crushed
1½ teaspoons five-spice powder
10cm stick (20g) fresh lemon grass,
  chopped finely
2cm piece fresh ginger (10g), grated
2 tablespoons peanut oil
1 medium brown onion (150g),
  sliced thinly

1 fresh long red chilli, chopped finely
1 medium red capsicum (200g),
  sliced thickly
⅓ cup (80ml) hoisin sauce
2 teaspoons finely grated lemon rind
1 tablespoon lemon juice
½ cup coarsely chopped fresh coriander
2 tablespoons fried shallots
1 green onion, sliced thinly

*Fried shallots are usually
served as a condiment on
the table or sprinkled over
cooked dishes. They can
be purchased packaged
in jars or cellophane bags
at all Asian grocery stores;
once opened, they keep
for months if stored tightly
sealed. Make your own
by frying thinly sliced
shallots until crisp and
golden-brown.*

1   Combine chicken with half the garlic, 1 teaspoon of the five-spice and all of
the lemon grass and ginger in large bowl. Cover, refrigerate 1 hour.
2   Heat half the oil in wok; stir-fry brown onion, chilli, capsicum and remaining garlic,
until onion softens. Remove from wok.
3   Heat remaining oil in wok; stir-fry chicken, in batches, until cooked.
4   Return onion mixture and chicken to wok with sauce, rind, juice and remaining
five-spice; stir-fry until sauce thickens slightly. Remove from heat; toss coriander
into stir-fry, sprinkle with shallots and green onion.
*per serving 15.4g total fat (3.1g saturated fat); 1601kJ (383 cal); 12.1g carbohydrate;
47.2g protein; 3.9g fibre*

sweet and sour duck with broccolini

PREPARATION TIME **25 MINUTES** COOKING TIME **10 MINUTES** SERVES **4**

1kg chinese barbecued duck
2 small red onions (200g), cut into
  thin wedges
1 fresh small red thai chilli, chopped finely
250g broccolini, cut into 3cm pieces
¼ cup (60ml) chicken stock

¼ cup (90g) honey
¼ cup (60ml) rice vinegar
1 tablespoon light soy sauce
2 teaspoons pomegranate molasses
4 green onions, cut into 3cm lengths
1 tablespoon sesame seeds, roasted

Pomegranate molasses is thicker, browner and more concentrated in flavour than grenadine, a sweet pomegranate syrup used in cocktails. Possessing tart and fruity qualities similar to balsamic vinegar, it is good brushed over grilling or roasting meat, seafood or poultry, and a spoonful in a salad dressing adds a gentle kick. Pomegranate molasses is available at Middle Eastern food stores and specialty food shops.

1 Quarter duck; discard bones. Slice duck meat thickly, keeping skin intact. Heat oiled wok; stir-fry duck, in batches, until skin is crisp.
2 Heat oiled wok; stir-fry red onion and chilli until onion softens slightly. Add broccolini, stock, honey, vinegar, sauce and molasses; stir-fry until sauce thickens slightly.
3 Remove from heat; serve broccolini mixture with duck and green onion; sprinkle with seeds.
per serving 38.9g total fat (11.3g saturated fat); 2437kJ (583 cal); 24.7g carbohydrate; 33g protein; 3.7g fibre

chicken and okra

PREPARATION TIME **25 MINUTES** COOKING TIME **15 MINUTES** SERVES **4**

2 tablespoons peanut oil

1kg chicken breast fillets, diced
  into 2cm pieces

350g okra, halved lengthways

1 medium brown onion (150g),
  sliced thinly

2 cloves garlic, crushed

2cm piece fresh ginger (10g), grated

¼ cup (75g) red curry paste

¼ cup (60ml) chicken stock

2 tablespoons lime juice

¾ cup loosely packed thai basil leaves

1 Heat 1 tablespoon of the oil in wok; stir-fry chicken, in batches, until cooked.

2 Heat half the remaining oil in wok; stir-fry okra until browned and tender. Remove from heat; cover to keep warm.

3 Heat remaining oil in wok; stir-fry onion, garlic and ginger until onion softens. Add curry paste; stir-fry about 1 minute or until fragrant.

4 Return chicken to wok with stock and juice; stir-fry 2 minutes. Remove from heat; stir in basil. Serve okra with chicken.

per serving 29.1g total fat (6.5g saturated fat); 2199kJ (526 cal); 4.7g carbohydrate; 58.3g protein; 6.4g fibre

sweet chilli plum chicken with noodles

PREPARATION TIME **20 MINUTES (PLUS REFRIGERATION TIME)** COOKING TIME **20 MINUTES** SERVES **4**

¼ cup (60ml) sweet chilli sauce
2 tablespoons plum sauce
750g chicken thigh fillets, sliced thinly
450g hokkien noodles
227g can water chestnuts, rinsed, halved

8 green onions, sliced thickly
1 fresh long red chilli, sliced thinly
2 cloves garlic, crushed
300g buk choy, trimmed,
  chopped coarsely

1 Combine sauces with chicken in large bowl. Cover; refrigerate 1 hour.

2 Heat oiled wok; stir-fry chicken mixture, in batches, until browned.

3 Meanwhile, place noodles in medium heatproof bowl; cover with boiling water, separate with fork, drain.

4 Stir-fry chestnuts, onion, chilli and garlic in wok 2 minutes. Return chicken to wok with buk choy; stir-fry until chicken is cooked. Serve with noodles.

per serving 14.9g total fat (4.2g saturated fat); 2011kJ (481 cal); 43.1g carbohydrate; 41g protein; 5.4g fibre

pad thai

PREPARATION TIME **20 MINUTES** COOKING TIME **10 MINUTES** SERVES **4**

200g dried rice stick noodles
2 cloves garlic, quartered
2 fresh small red thai chillies,
  chopped coarsely
2 tablespoons peanut oil
2 eggs, beaten lightly
1 cup (80g) fried shallots
125g packet fried tofu, cut into
  2cm cubes

¼ cup (35g) roasted unsalted peanuts,
  chopped coarsely
3 cups (240g) bean sprouts
6 green onions, sliced thinly
2 tablespoons light soy sauce
1 tablespoon lime juice
2 tablespoons coarsely chopped
  fresh coriander

1 Place noodles in large heatproof bowl, cover with boiling water; stand until just tender, drain.
2 Meanwhile, using mortar and pestle, crush garlic and chilli to a paste.
3 Heat 2 teaspoons of the oil in wok. Pour egg into wok; cook over medium heat, tilting pan, until almost set. Remove omelette from wok; roll tightly, slice thinly.
4 Heat remaining oil in wok, stir-fry garlic paste and shallots until fragrant. Add tofu; stir-fry 1 minute. Add half the nuts, half the sprouts and half the onion; stir-fry until spouts are just wilted.
5 Add noodles, sauce and juice; stir-fry until hot. Remove from heat; sprinkle omelette, coriander and remaining nuts, sprouts and onion over pad thai.
per serving 19.6g total fat (3.4g saturated fat); 1246kJ (298 cal); 15.1g carbohydrate; 13.4g protein; 4.3g fibre

hot, sweet and sour mixed vegetables

PREPARATION TIME **20 MINUTES** COOKING TIME **10 MINUTES** SERVES **4**

1 tablespoon peanut oil
3cm piece fresh ginger (15g), grated
2 cloves garlic, crushed
2 fresh small red thai chillies,
  chopped finely
1 medium red capsicum (200g),
  sliced thinly
1 medium yellow capsicum (200g),
  sliced thinly
230g fresh baby corn, halved lengthways
¼ cup (60ml) vegetable stock

2 tablespoons vegetarian mushroom
  oyster sauce
2 tablespoons grated palm sugar
2 tablespoons tamarind concentrate
350g baby buk choy, chopped coarsely
280g gai lan, chopped coarsely
150g oyster mushrooms,
  chopped coarsely
6 green onions, cut into 3cm lengths
½ cup firmly packed vietnamese
  mint leaves

1   Heat oil in wok; stir-fry ginger, garlic and chilli until fragrant. Add capsicums and corn; stir-fry until tender. Add stock, sauce, sugar and tamarind; stir-fry 2 minutes.
2   Add buk choy, gai lan and mushrooms to wok; stir-fry until greens wilt. Remove from heat; stir in onion and mint.
per serving 6.1g total fat (1g saturated fat); 861kJ (206 cal); 25.8g carbohydrate; 7.9g protein; 8.5g fibre

north african chickpea, okra and cauliflower with couscous

PREPARATION TIME **5 MINUTES**   COOKING TIME **20 MINUTES**   SERVES **4**

2 tablespoons olive oil
250g cauliflower, cut into florets
1 clove garlic, crushed
2 teaspoons ground cumin
1 teaspoon ground coriander
¼ teaspoon cayenne pepper
250g okra, halved lengthways
⅔ cup (160ml) vegetable stock
420g can chickpeas, rinsed, drained
300g greek-style yogurt
2 tablespoons finely chopped
  preserved lemon

COUSCOUS
1½ cups (375ml) water
2 teaspoons olive oil
1½ cups (300g) couscous
¼ cup finely chopped fresh
  flat-leaf parsley
¼ cup (40g) roasted pine nuts

1   Heat oil in wok; stir-fry cauliflower, garlic and spices about 2 minutes or until mixture is fragrant and cauliflower slightly tender. Add okra and stock; stir-fry about 5 minutes or until okra is just tender. Add chickpeas; stir-fry until hot.
2   Meanwhile, make couscous; cover to keep warm.
3   Serve couscous topped with vegetables and combined yogurt and lemon.
COUSCOUS Bring the water and oil to a boil in large saucepan; remove from heat. Add couscous; cover, stand about 5 minutes or until water is absorbed, fluffing occasionally with fork. Stir in parsley and nuts.
per serving 26g total fat (5.8g saturated fat); 2730kJ (653 cal); 76.9g carbohydrate; 23.3g protein; 8.4g fibre

crispy shredded beef

PREPARATION TIME **30 MINUTES**   COOKING TIME **2 HOURS (PLUS STANDING TIME)**   SERVES **4**

750g piece corned silverside
1 litre (4 cups) milk, approximately
1 fresh long red chilli, chopped coarsely
2 kaffir lime leaves, torn
3cm piece fresh ginger (15g),
   chopped coarsely
2 cloves garlic, quartered
450g wide fresh rice noodles
¼ cup (60ml) peanut oil
1 fresh small red thai chilli, sliced thinly

3 cloves garlic, crushed
3cm piece fresh ginger (15g), grated
1 medium red capsicum (200g),
   sliced thinly
150g sugar snap peas, trimmed
1 tablespoon fish sauce
2 tablespoons kecap manis
½ cup loosely packed fresh
   coriander leaves

*Corned silverside is
beef that is first pickled
in brine then cooked
submerged in water
with spices, herbs, etc.
Here we poach the
silverside in milk to
draw out as much
salt as possible.*

1   Place beef with as much milk as needed to cover it in large saucepan; bring to a boil. Reduce heat; simmer, uncovered, 10 minutes. Drain beef; discard milk.
2   Place beef, chopped chilli, lime leaves, chopped ginger and quartered garlic in same cleaned pan. Cover with cold water; simmer, covered, 1½ hours. Remove beef from pan; discard pan ingredients. Drain beef on wire rack over tray 15 minutes.
3   Meanwhile, place noodles in large heatproof bowl, cover with boiling water; separate with fork, drain.
4   Trim excess fat from beef. Using two forks, shred beef finely. Heat oil in wok; stir-fry beef, in batches, until browned and crisp. Drain.
5   Stir-fry sliced chilli, crushed garlic, grated ginger, capsicum and peas in wok until vegetables soften. Add sauces; stir-fry 1 minute.
6   Return beef to wok with noodles; stir-fry until hot. Remove from heat; sprinkle with coriander.

per serving 29.4g total fat (11.2g saturated fat); 2571kJ (615 cal); 41g carbohydrate; 45.8g protein; 2.8g fibre

hokkien mee with beef

PREPARATION TIME 15 MINUTES COOKING TIME 15 MINUTES SERVES 4

Hokkein (or Fukkian) food is one of the many regional cuisines that go into the array of dishes that together become Singaporean food. The Hokkiens are originally from the southeast coast of China and, although many Hokkiens now live in Singapore, their food is seldom seen in restaurants because of its simplicity and homeliness. One dish that has become an international hit, however, is hokkien fried noodles – and this recipe shows why.

300g hokkien noodles
1 tablespoon peanut oil
700g beef rump steak, sliced thinly
1 medium brown onion (150g), sliced thinly
3cm piece fresh ginger (15g), grated
2 cloves garlic, crushed

2 fresh red thai chillies, sliced thinly
1 small red capsicum (150g), sliced thinly
1 small green capsicum (150g), sliced thinly
200g mushrooms, quartered
2 tablespoons hoisin sauce
1 tablespoon dark soy sauce

1 Place noodles in medium heatproof bowl, cover with boiling water; separate with fork, drain.
2 Heat half the oil in wok; stir-fry beef, in batches, until browned.
3 Heat remaining oil in wok; stir-fry onion until soft. Add ginger, garlic and chilli; stir-fry until fragrant. Add capsicums and mushrooms; stir-fry until tender.
4 Return beef to wok with noodles and sauces; stir-fry until hot.
per serving 17.4g total fat (6.2g saturated fat); 1927kJ (461 cal); 27.2g carbohydrate; 46.1g protein; 5.3g fibre

SHORT-ORDER

asian greens with garlic
Stir-fried asian greens make a healthy accompaniment to meat dishes. Firstly, trim and discard the stems and unsightly leaves from buk choy, choy sum and wombok. Separate the leaves then stir-fry with some crushed garlic and grated ginger until the greens just wilt.

honey and five-spice beef with broccolini

PREPARATION TIME **10 MINUTES (PLUS REFRIGERATION TIME)** COOKING TIME **15 MINUTES** SERVES **4**

1 teaspoon five-spice powder
4cm fresh ginger (20g), grated
750g beef strips
2 tablespoons peanut oil
¼ cup (60ml) dark soy sauce

2 tablespoons honey
2 teaspoons lemon juice
350g broccolini, chopped coarsely
⅓ cup (35g) walnuts, chopped coarsely
1 tablespoon roasted sesame seeds

1   Combine five-spice, ginger, beef and half the oil in large bowl. Cover; refrigerate 1 hour.
2   Heat remaining oil in wok; stir-fry beef, in batches, until browned.
3   Add sauce, honey and juice to wok; bring to a boil. Simmer, 2 minutes.
4   Return beef to wok with broccolini; stir-fry until broccolini is tender. Remove from heat; sprinkle with nuts and seeds.
per serving 28.1g total fat (6.9g saturated fat); 2077kJ (497 cal); 12.8g carbohydrate; 46.7g protein; 4.6g fibre

lemon veal with asian greens

PREPARATION TIME **10 MINUTES** COOKING TIME **15 MINUTES** SERVES **4**

2 tablespoons vegetable oil
750g veal strips
10cm stick (20g) fresh lemon grass,
  chopped finely
500g baby buk choy, trimmed,
  quartered lengthways
500g choy sum, trimmed,
  halved crossways

2 cloves garlic, crushed
2 teaspoons finely grated lemon rind
¼ cup (60ml) lemon juice
¼ cup (60ml) dark soy sauce
4 green onions, sliced thinly
⅓ cup (55g) roasted almonds,
  chopped coarsely

1   Heat half the oil in wok; stir-fry veal, in batches, until browned.
2   Heat remaining oil in wok; stir-fry lemon grass until fragrant. Add buk choy, choy sum, garlic, rind, juice and sauce; stir-fry until vegetables wilt.
3   Return veal to wok with onion; stir-fry until hot. Remove from heat; sprinkle with nuts.
per serving 20.2g total fat (2.4g saturated fat); 1705kJ (408 cal); 4.6g carbohydrate; 48.6g protein; 5.1g fibre

peppercorn beef

PREPARATION TIME **20 MINUTES (PLUS REFRIGERATION TIME)** COOKING TIME **20 MINUTES** SERVES **4**

2 tablespoons dark soy sauce
3cm piece fresh ginger (15g), grated
2 cloves garlic, crushed
2 teaspoons cornflour
1 teaspoon sesame oil
800g beef rump steak, sliced thinly
2 teaspoons pepper medley
¼ teaspoon sichuan peppercorns

2 tablespoons peanut oil
1 medium brown onion (150g),
 sliced thinly
150g snake beans, chopped coarsely
2 tablespoons chinese cooking wine
½ cup (125ml) water
2 tablespoons oyster sauce
4 green onions, sliced thickly

*Pepper medley is
a mixture of black,
white, green and pink
peppercorns, coriander
seeds and allspice,
sold in grinders in
supermarkets. You can
use your own blend of
various peppercorns,
if you prefer.*

1 Combine soy sauce, ginger, garlic, cornflour and sesame oil in large bowl;
add beef, mix well. Cover; refrigerate 1 hour.
2 Meanwhile, using mortar and pestle, crush pepper medley and sichuan
peppercorns finely.
3 Heat half the peanut oil in wok; stir-fry beef, in batches, until browned.
4 Heat remaining oil in wok; stir-fry brown onion, beans and pepper mixture until
onion is tender. Return beef to wok with wine, the water and oyster sauce; bring to
a boil. Stir-fry until beans are cooked. Remove from heat; stir in green onion.
*per serving 24g total fat (7.8g saturated fat); 1889kJ (452 cal); 7.6g carbohydrate;
47.8g protein; 2.1g fibre*

larb lamb

PREPARATION TIME **20 MINUTES** COOKING TIME **15 MINUTES** SERVES **4**

1 tablespoon peanut oil
5cm stick (10g) fresh lemon grass,
 chopped finely
2 fresh small red thai chillies,
 chopped finely
2 cloves garlic, crushed
3cm piece fresh ginger (15g),
 chopped finely
750g lamb mince
1 lebanese cucumber (130g), seeded,
 sliced thinly
1 small red onion (100g), sliced thinly
1 cup (80g) bean sprouts
½ cup loosely packed thai basil leaves
1 cup loosely packed fresh coriander leaves
8 large iceberg lettuce leaves

DRESSING
⅓ cup (80ml) lime juice
2 tablespoons fish sauce
2 tablespoons kecap manis
2 tablespoons peanut oil
2 teaspoons grated palm sugar
½ teaspoon sambal oelek

One of the vast family of classic Thai warm salads, larb is distinguished from the others by the presence of mince as its main ingredient. Whether it's tofu, meat or seafood – or even a few vegetables and fruits – the main ingredient in larb is always chopped or minced, and served with fresh herbs, leafy greens and other vegetables.

1 Place ingredients for dressing in screw-top jar; shake well.
2 Heat oil in wok; stir-fry lemon grass, chilli, garlic and ginger until fragrant.
3 Add lamb; stir-fry, in batches, until changed in colour.
4 Return lamb to wok with a third of the dressing; stir-fry about 2 minutes or until most of the liquid has evaporated.
5 Place remaining dressing in large bowl with lamb mixture, cucumber, onion, sprouts and herbs; toss larb to combine. Serve larb in lettuce leaves.
per serving 26.9g total fat (8.3g saturated fat); 1852kJ (443 cal); 6.1g carbohydrate; 42.1g protein; 3.7g fibre

balinese chilli lamb and fried noodles

PREPARATION TIME **15 MINUTES** COOKING TIME **10 MINUTES** SERVES **4**

600g hokkien noodles
1 tablespoon sambal oelek
1 tablespoon dark soy sauce
1 tablespoon fish sauce
2 cloves garlic, crushed
750g lamb backstraps, sliced thinly
¼ cup (60ml) peanut oil
⅓ cup (55g) coarsely chopped
  brazil nuts

⅔ cup (160ml) beef stock
2 tablespoons oyster sauce
2 tablespoons lime juice
2 teaspoons brown sugar
150g sugar snap peas, trimmed
⅓ cup finely chopped fresh mint
2 fresh small red thai chillies,
  chopped finely

1   Place noodles in large heatproof bowl, cover with boiling water;
separate with fork, drain.
2   Combine sambal, sauces and garlic in large bowl with lamb.
3   Heat half a teaspoon of oil in wok; stir-fry nuts until browned lightly.
Remove from wok.
4   Heat 2 tablespoons of remaining oil in wok; stir-fry lamb, in batches,
until browned.
5   Heat remaining oil in wok; stir-fry noodles until browned lightly.
6   Add stock, oyster sauce, juice and sugar to wok; simmer about
3 minutes or until sauce thickens slightly.
7   Return lamb to wok with peas; stir-fry until hot. Serve noodles
topped with lamb mixture and sprinkled with nuts, mint and chilli.
*per serving 40.5g total fat (12.1g saturated fat); 3164kJ (757 cal); 45.4g carbohydrate;
50.2g protein; 5.4g fibre*

turkish lamb, mint and spinach

PREPARATION TIME **15 MINUTES** COOKING TIME **15 MINUTES** SERVES **4**

2 tablespoons vegetable oil
½ cup (80g) pine nuts
750g lamb strips
1 large brown onion (200g),
  chopped coarsely
2 cloves garlic, crushed
2 fresh small red thai chillies,
  chopped finely

1 tablespoon ground coriander
1 tablespoon ground cumin
300g spinach, trimmed,
  chopped coarsely
¼ cup coarsely chopped fresh mint
4 large pittas (330g)
400g yogurt
2 tablespoons lemon juice

1   Heat 2 teaspoons of the oil in wok; stir-fry nuts until browned. Drain.
2   Heat 1 tablespoon of remaining oil in wok; stir-fry lamb, in batches, until browned.
3   Heat remaining oil in wok; stir-fry onion, garlic and chilli until onion softens. Add spices; stir-fry until fragrant.
4   Return lamb to wok with nuts, spinach and mint; stir-fry until spinach wilts and lamb is cooked.
5   Serve pitta topped with lamb then combined yogurt and juice.
per serving 45.4g total fat (12g saturated fat); 3570kJ (854 cal); 50.9g carbohydrate; 56.8g protein; 6.4g fibre

PORK

Perfect for stir-fries, full-flavoured pork is popular in many Asian dishes

chilli orange pork

PREPARATION TIME 15 MINUTES COOKING TIME 15 MINUTES SERVES 6

2 tablespoons peanut oil
1kg pork fillets, sliced thinly
1 medium brown onion (150g),
  chopped coarsely
2 cloves garlic, crushed
1 fresh long red chilli, chopped finely

250g sugar snap peas, trimmed
¼ cup (60ml) light soy sauce
⅓ cup (80ml) sweet sherry
2 teaspoons finely grated orange rind
2 tablespoons orange juice
1 teaspoon cornflour

1 Heat half the oil in wok; stir-fry pork, in batches, until browned.
2 Heat remaining oil in wok; stir-fry onion, garlic and chilli until onion softens.
Add peas; stir-fry until peas are just tender.
3 Return pork to wok with sauce, sherry, rind and blended juice and cornflour;
stir-fry until sauce thickens slightly.
per serving 10g total fat (2.4g saturated fat); 1195kJ (286 cal); 5.9g carbohydrate;
38.8g protein; 1.5g fibre

curried fried rice with pork and prawns

PREPARATION TIME **20 MINUTES** COOKING TIME **25 MINUTES** SERVES **4**

800g pork leg steaks, sliced thinly
1 tablespoon white sugar
2 tablespoons light soy sauce
125g uncooked small prawns
2 tablespoons peanut oil
2 eggs, beaten lightly

1 teaspoon curry powder
2 cloves garlic, crushed
2 cups cold cooked white long-grain rice
4 green onions, sliced thinly
2 cups (240g) frozen peas and corn

*Packages of mixed
frozen peas and
corn are found in
most supermarkets.
You need to cook
approximately ⅔ cup
of rice for this recipe.*

1 Combine pork in medium bowl with sugar and half the sauce. Shell and devein prawns, leaving tails intact.

2 Heat 1 teaspoon of the oil in wok. Pour egg into wok; cook over medium heat, tilting wok, until almost set. Remove omelette from wok; roll tightly, slice thinly.

3 Heat 2 teaspoons of the remaining oil in wok; stir-fry pork, in batches, until cooked as desired.

4 Heat 1 teaspoon of remaining oil in wok; stir-fry prawns until just changed in colour. Remove from wok.

5 Heat remaining oil in wok; cook curry powder and garlic, stirring, until fragrant. Add rice, onion, pea and corn mixture and remaining sauce; stir-fry until vegetables are just tender.

6 Return pork, prawns and half of the omelette to wok; stir-fry until heated through. Sprinkle fried rice with remaining omelette.

per serving 18.1g total fat (4.3g saturated fat); 2337kJ (559 cal); 38g carbohydrate; 57.5g protein; 4.9g fibre

grandma's tofu

PREPARATION TIME **15 MINUTES** COOKING TIME **15 MINUTES** SERVES **4**

Frequently found on Chinese restaurant menus as "mapo tofu", this recipe is one of the most universally popular tofu dishes. We used cryovac-packed ready-to-serve sweet chilli tofu cubes, available from most supermarkets and Asian food stores. Tamari is a thick, dark soy sauce.

2 tablespoons peanut oil
½ cup (80g) coarsely chopped almonds
1 medium brown onion (150g), chopped finely
500g pork mince
150g mushrooms, sliced thinly

200g packaged marinated tofu pieces
2 tablespoons sambal oelek
1 tablespoon kecap manis
2 tablespoons tamari
¼ cup (60ml) lime juice
4 green onions, sliced thinly

1 Heat half the oil in wok; stir-fry nuts until browned. Drain.
2 Heat remaining oil in wok; stir-fry brown onion until just soft. Add pork; stir-fry, in batches, until cooked.
3 Return pork and onion to wok. Add mushrooms and tofu; stir-fry until mushrooms are just tender. Add sambal, kecap manis and tamari; stir-fry until sauce thickens slightly. Remove from heat; serve stir-fry sprinkled with nuts, juice and green onion.
per serving 32.6g total fat (6.1g saturated fat); 2011kJ (481 cal); 6.9g carbohydrate; 38g protein; 4.3g fibre

quick pork fried rice

PREPARATION TIME **20 MINUTES** COOKING TIME **15 MINUTES** SERVES **4**

You need to cook approximately 1 cup of rice for this recipe.

600g pork fillets, sliced thinly
1 tablespoon honey
2 tablespoons kecap manis
2 teaspoons peanut oil
2 eggs, beaten lightly
1 medium carrot (120g), cut into matchstick-sized pieces

1 medium red capsicum (200g), sliced thinly
3 cups cold cooked white long-grain rice
8 green onions, sliced thinly
1 cup (80g) bean sprouts
2 tablespoons soy sauce
2 tablespoons char siu sauce

1 Combine pork in medium bowl with honey and kecap manis.
2 Heat half the oil in wok. Pour egg into wok; cook over medium heat, tilting pan, until almost set. Remove omelette from wok; roll tightly, slice thinly.
3 Heat remaining oil in wok; stir-fry pork, in batches, until cooked.
4 Stir-fry carrot and capsicum in wok until just tender.
5 Return half the omelette to wok with rice, pork, onion, sprouts and sauces; stir-fry until hot. Remove from heat; sprinkle with remaining omelette.
per serving 9.4g total fat (2.5g saturated fat); 2032kJ (486 cal); 54.6g carbohydrate; 42.6g protein; 4.7g fibre

SHORT-ORDER

stuffed tofu triangles
Another Chinese recipe
that mixes tofu and pork is
stuffed bean curd. Cut large
rectangular pieces of tofu
in half diagonally to form
triangles, then scoop out
some of the tofu centre.
Chop an onion and some
garlic, mix them with pork
mince and stuff into the
hollowed-out tofu. Steam
or fry tofu triangles until
the filling is cooked.

chiang mai pork and eggplant

PREPARATION TIME **20 MINUTES** COOKING TIME **25 MINUTES** SERVES **4**

3 fresh small red thai chillies, halved
6 cloves garlic, quartered
1 medium brown onion (150g),
  chopped coarsely
500g baby eggplants
¼ cup (60ml) peanut oil
700g pork leg steaks, sliced thinly

1 tablespoon fish sauce
1 tablespoon dark soy sauce
1 tablespoon grated palm sugar
4 purple thai shallots (100g), sliced thinly
150g snake beans, cut into 5cm lengths
1 cup loosely packed thai basil leaves

*The food of Chiang
Mai in the northwest
of Thailand is hearty,
pungent and highly
spiced. Its style is
identifiable by the
use of a thick garlic
and chilli paste stir-fried
with vegetables.
Thai purple shallots,
also known as pink
shallots or homm, are
used all over South-East
Asia. While good used
in cooking, they also
can be eaten raw
in salads or deep-fried
as a condiment.*

1   Blend or process chilli, garlic and onion until mixture forms a paste.
2   Quarter eggplants lengthways; slice each piece into 5cm lengths. Cook eggplant in large saucepan of boiling water until just tender; drain, pat dry.
3   Heat half the oil in wok; stir-fry eggplant, in batches, until browned lightly. Drain.
4   Heat remaining oil in wok; stir-fry pork, in batches, until cooked.
5   Stir-fry garlic paste in wok about 3 minutes or until fragrant and browned lightly. Add sauces and sugar; stir-fry until sugar dissolves.
6   Add shallot and beans; stir-fry until beans are tender. Return eggplant and pork to wok; stir-fry until hot. Remove from heat; sprinkle with basil.
per serving 19.3g total fat (4.1g saturated fat); 1672kJ (400 cal); 10.1g carbohydrate; 43.6g protein; 5.8g fibre

sticky pork with vegies

PREPARATION TIME **15 MINUTES (PLUS REFRIGERATION TIME)** COOKING TIME **25 MINUTES** SERVES **4**

1 tablespoon honey

2 tablespoons light soy sauce

2 tablespoons brown sugar

1 teaspoon five-spice powder

1 teaspoon hot chilli powder

3 cloves garlic, crushed

1 teaspoon sesame oil

750g pork neck, cut into 3cm cubes

2 tablespoons peanut oil

½ cup (70g) raw peanuts,
   chopped coarsely

1 medium carrot (120g), cut
   into matchsticks

150g snow peas, trimmed,
   sliced thinly lengthways

2 tablespoons orange juice

3 kaffir lime leaves, shredded

4 green onions, sliced thinly

1   Combine honey, sauce, sugar, five-spice, chilli, garlic and sesame oil in large bowl; add pork, turn to coat in marinade. Cover; refrigerate 3 hours or overnight.

2   Heat half the peanut oil in wok; stir-fry nuts until browned. Drain.

3   Heat remaining oil in wok. Add pork; stir-fry, in batches, until browned. Return pork to wok with carrot; stir-fry until pork is cooked.

4   Add snow peas, juice and lime leaves; stir-fry until snow peas are tender. Remove from heat; toss in onion and nuts.

per serving 33.7g total fat (8.1g saturated fat); 2366kJ (566 cal); 18.5g carbohydrate; 46.4g protein; 3.8g fibre

SHORT-ORDER

sweet and sour baked fish
Sweet and sour are two flavours considered essential by the Chinese for a well-balanced meal. However, combining the two in one dish is thought to have been an attempt to cater to the European palate. You can marry sweet and sour sauce with anything from beef to seafood. For a quick and easy dinner, bake a whole fish, such as snapper, in the oven for about half an hour or until browned and cooked through. While it is baking, make a sauce using the water, garlic, sugar, vinegar and sauces on the page opposite. Spoon it over the fish and serve with steamed green vegetables.

sang choy bow

PREPARATION TIME **15 MINUTES** COOKING TIME **15 MINUTES** SERVES **4**

The size of the butter lettuce available will determine whether you buy one or two of them in order to get a dozen large leaves. You could also use large iceberg leaves.

2 teaspoons sesame oil
1 small brown onion (80g), chopped finely
2 cloves garlic, crushed
2cm piece fresh ginger (10g), grated
500g lean pork mince
2 tablespoons water
100g shiitake mushrooms, chopped finely

2 tablespoons light soy sauce
2 tablespoons oyster sauce
1 tablespoon lime juice
2 cups bean sprouts
4 green onions, sliced thinly
¼ cup coarsely chopped fresh coriander
12 large butter lettuce leaves

1   Heat oil in wok; stir-fry brown onion, garlic and ginger until onion softens. Add pork; stir-fry until changed in colour.
2   Add the water, mushrooms, sauces and juice; stir-fry until mushrooms are tender. Remove from heat. Add sprouts, green onion and coriander; toss to combine.
3   Spoon sang choy bow into lettuce leaves to serve.
per serving 11.5g total fat (3.6g saturated fat); 1112kJ (266 cal); 8.9g carbohydrate; 29.3g protein; 4.1g fibre

pork with sweet and sour peaches

PREPARATION TIME **20 MINUTES** COOKING TIME **10 MINUTES** SERVES **4**

2 tablespoons cornflour
800g pork fillets, sliced thinly
2 tablespoons peanut oil
1 medium red onion (170g), chopped coarsely
1 medium red capsicum (200g), cut into thin strips
1 medium yellow capsicum (200g), cut into thin strips

⅓ cup (80ml) water
2 cloves garlic, crushed
2 tablespoons white sugar
2 tablespoons white wine vinegar
2 tablespoons tomato sauce
2 tablespoons light soy sauce
2 large peaches (440g), cut into wedges
⅓ cup coarsely chopped fresh coriander

1   Rub cornflour into pork in medium bowl.
2   Heat half the oil in wok; stir-fry pork, in batches, until browned.
3   Heat remaining oil in same wok; stir-fry onion and capsicums until tender.
4   Return pork to wok with the water, garlic, sugar, vinegar and sauces; stir-fry until pork is cooked. Add peach; stir-fry until hot. Remove from heat; toss in coriander.
per serving 25.4g total fat (7.1g saturated fat); 2203kJ (527 cal); 26.9g carbohydrate; 45.9g protein; 3g fibre

fried noodles with sausage and cabbage

PREPARATION TIME **25 MINUTES** COOKING TIME **10 MINUTES** SERVES **4**

450g wide fresh rice noodles
2 teaspoons peanut oil
300g dried chinese sausages,
　sliced thickly
1 medium brown onion (150g),
　chopped coarsely
2 cloves garlic, crushed
100g shiitake mushrooms,
　chopped coarsely
1 small wombok (700g),
　chopped coarsely

¼ cup (60ml) chicken stock
¼ cup (95g) char siu sauce
2 tablespoons lime juice
½ cup loosely packed fresh
　coriander leaves
¼ cup loosely packed fresh mint leaves
⅓ cup (50g) coarsely chopped roasted
　unsalted cashews
1 fresh long red chilli, sliced thinly

1　Place noodles in large heatproof bowl, cover with boiling water; separate with fork, drain.

2　Heat oil in wok; stir-fry sausage, onion, garlic and mushrooms until sausage is browned and vegetables tender.

3　Add wombok; stir-fry until wombok wilts. Add stock, sauce, juice and noodles; stir-fry until hot. Remove from heat; sprinkle with coriander and mint. Serve with nuts and chilli.

per serving 28.4g total fat (7.8g saturated fat); 2161kJ (517 cal); 43.6g carbohydrate; 17.6g protein; 9.8g fibre

twice-cooked pork

PREPARATION TIME **15 MINUTES**   COOKING TIME **1 HOUR 10 MINUTES (PLUS COOLING AND STANDING TIME)**   SERVES **4**

800g pork belly, skin removed
4cm piece fresh ginger (20g), grated
2 green onions, chopped coarsely
1 tablespoon vegetable oil
1 medium red capsicum (200g),
   sliced thinly
1 medium green capsicum (200g),
   sliced thinly

1 medium yellow capsicum (200g),
   sliced thinly
2 cloves garlic, crushed
¼ cup (60ml) hoisin sauce
2 tablespoons dark soy sauce
1 tablespoon lime juice
¼ teaspoon chilli flakes
3 green onions, sliced thinly

"Twice-cooked" Chinese dishes date from days before refrigeration, when people boiled large cuts of meat because it kept better than if left fresh. Here, it also serves the purpose of ridding the meat of some of its excess fat. For extra-crisp pork, serve it on the capsicum mixture rather than tossing them together.

1   Place pork, ginger and chopped onion in wok; cover with cold water. Bring to a boil then simmer, uncovered, 30 minutes. Cool pork in water; drain.
2   Place pork on tray; stand about 20 minutes or until completely dried. Slice thinly.
3   Heat oil in cleaned wok; stir-fry pork, in batches, until crisp. Drain; cover to keep warm.
4   Reserve about 2 teaspoons of the oil in wok; discard remainder. Add capsicums and garlic to wok; stir-fry until tender. Stir in sauces, juice and chilli. Serve capsicum topped with pork and sprinkled with sliced onion.
per serving 50.3g total fat (15.9g saturated fat); 2738kJ (655 cal); 11.1g carbohydrate; 39.3g protein; 3.6g fibre

GLOSSARY

BAMBOO SHOOTS the tender shoots of bamboo plants, available in cans; must be drained and rinsed before use.

BEAN SPROUTS also known as bean shoots; tender new growths of assorted beans and seeds germinated for consumption as sprouts. The most readily available are mung bean, soy bean, alfalfa and snow pea sprouts.

BROCCOLINI a cross between broccoli and chinese kale; is milder and sweeter than traditional broccoli. Substitute gai lan (chinese broccoli) or common broccoli.

BUK CHOY also known as bok choy, bak choy, pak choy and chinese white cabbage; has a mild mustard taste. *Baby buk choy* is smaller, more tender and less peppery than buk choy.

CAPSICUM also known as bell pepper or, simply, pepper; come in many colours. Discard seeds and membranes before use.

CAYENNE PEPPER a thin-fleshed, long, extremely hot dried red chilli; usually purchased ground.

CHEESE
haloumi a firm, cream-coloured sheep-milk cheese matured in brine; somewhat like a minty, salty fetta in flavour, haloumi can be grilled or fried, briefly, without breaking down.
paneer (or panir) a fresh unripened, unsalted, cow-milk cheese similar to pressed ricotta. Does not melt at normal cooking temperatures. It is used in curried dishes or to make sweets; available in supermarkets.

CHICKPEAS also called garbanzos, hummus or channa; an irregularly round, sandy-coloured legume.

CHILLI available in many different types, fresh or dried. Use rubber gloves when seeding and chopping fresh chillies, as they can burn your skin. Removing seeds and membranes lessens the heat level.
jam an aromatic, spicy sauce made from chilli, garlic, onion, shallot, tomato puree, fish sauce, tamarind and other asian seasonings; sold, bottled, in supermarkets.

long red medium-sized, moderately hot chillies.
sauce and **sweet chilli sauce** (see sauces).
thai red small, hot, red chillies.

CHINESE BARBECUED DUCK has a sweet-sticky coating made from hoisin sauce, soy sauce, five-spice and sherry. Available from Asian food stores.

CHINESE BARBECUED PORK also called char siew. Has a sweet-sticky coating made from soy sauce, sherry, five-spice powder and hoisin sauce. Available from Asian food stores.

CHINESE COOKING WINE made from rice, wheat, sugar and salt, with 13.5% alcohol; available from Asian food stores. Mirin or sherry can be substituted.

CHINESE SAUSAGES, DRIED also called lop chong; most commonly made from pork, but can be made with duck liver or beef. Red-brown in colour and sweet-spicy in flavour, they are sold, dried and strung, in all Asian food stores.

CHOY SUM also known as pakaukeo or flowering cabbage; easy to identify with its long stems, light green leaves and yellow flowers. It is eaten, stems and all, steamed or stir-fried.

CIABATTA in Italian the word means slipper, the traditional shape of this popular crisp-crusted white bread.

COCONUT CREAM is obtained commercially from the first pressing of the coconut flesh alone, without the addition of water. Available in cans and cartons at supermarkets.

CORIANDER also known as cilantro or chinese parsley; bright-green-leafed herb with a pungent flavour. Often stirred into or sprinkled over a dish just before serving for maximum impact. Both the stems and roots of coriander are also used in Thai cooking; wash well before chopping.

CORNFLOUR a thickening agent also known as cornstarch.

COUSCOUS a fine, grain-like cereal product, originally from North Africa; made from semolina.

CUMIN also known as zeera; available ground or as seeds from supermarkets.

CURRY
leaves used to add a spicy taste to many Asian foods. When added to hot oil, fresh curry leaves cause spattering; dried curry leaves are easier to cook, but burn easily. Fresh curry leaves can be found in Asian supermarkets and will keep for several weeks in plastic bags in the refrigerator. Dried curry leaves keep indefinitely in an airtight container, but the fresher they are, the better the flavour will be.
paste many prepared curry pastes are available in supermarkets and include green, red, yellow, panang and massaman curry pastes.

EGG if a recipe calls for raw or barely cooked eggs, exercise caution if there is a salmonella problem in your area.

EGGPLANT also known as aubergine.

FENNEL also known as finocchio or anise. Also the name given to dried seeds having a licorice flavour.

FIVE-SPICE POWDER a fragrant mixture of ground cinnamon, cloves, star anise, sichuan peppercorns and fennel seeds. Also known as chinese five-spice.

FLOUR, PLAIN an all-purpose flour made from wheat.

FRIED SHALLOTS served as a condiment or sprinkled over just-cooked food to provide an extra crunchy finish. Available from Asian grocery stores; once opened, will keep for months if stored in a tightly sealed glass jar.

GAI LAN also known as gai larn, gai lum, kanah, chinese broccoli and chinese kale; appreciated more for its stems than its coarse leaves.

GINGER when fresh, it is also known as green or root ginger. Can be kept, peeled, covered with dry sherry in a jar and refrigerated, or frozen in an airtight container.

GOLDEN SYRUP a by-product of refined sugarcane; pure maple syrup or honey can be substituted.

KAFFIR LIME LEAVES also known as bai magrood; look like two glossy dark green leaves joined end to end, forming a rounded hourglass shape. Sold fresh, dried or frozen, the dried leaves are less potent so double the number called for in a recipe if you substitute them for fresh leaves. A strip of fresh lime peel may be substituted for each kaffir lime leaf.

KALAMATA OLIVES small, sharp-tasting brine-cured black olives; available from major supermarkets and delicatessens.

KECAP ASIN and kecap manis (see sauces).

LEBANESE CUCUMBER slender, short and thin-skinned; also known as continental cucumber.

LEMON GRASS a tall, clumping, lemon-smelling and tasting, sharp-edged grass; the white lower part of each stem is chopped and used.

MINCE also known as ground meat.

MIRIN a champagne-coloured japanese cooking wine made of glutinous rice and alcohol expressly for cooking; should not be confused with sake.

MUSHROOMS
button common variety of small cultivated mushroom, sometimes called cap mushrooms.
enoki long, thin, white mushrooms, with a delicate fruit flavour.
oyster also known as abalone; grey-white mushroom shaped like a fan. Prized for their smooth texture and subtle, oyster-like flavour.
shiitake when fresh are also known as chinese black, forest or golden oak mushrooms; although cultivated, they have the earthiness and taste of wild mushrooms. When dried, they are known as donko or dried chinese mushrooms; rehydrate before use.

MUSTARD
dijon a pale brown, distinctively flavoured, fairly mild french mustard.
seeds, black also known as brown mustard seeds; more pungent than the white (or yellow) seeds used in most prepared mustards.

NOODLES
egg also known as ba mee or yellow noodles; made from wheat flour and eggs, sold fresh and dried. Range in size from very fine strands to wide, thick spaghetti-like pieces.
fresh rice also known as ho fun, khao pun, sen yau, kway tiau or pho depending on the country of manufacture; can be purchased in various widths or large sheets weighing about 500g, which are cut into the noodle-width desired. Chewy and pure white, they do not need pre-cooking before use.
fried crispy egg noodles that are already deep-fried, and packaged in a 100g packet.
hokkien also known as stir-fry noodles; fresh wheat flour noodles resembling thick, yellow-brown spaghetti, require heating, not cooking.
rice stick also known as sen lek, ho fun or kway teow. Should be soaked in hot water until soft.
soba thin japanese noodles made from a mix of buckwheat flour and wheat flour.
udon available fresh and dried, these broad, japanese white wheat noodles are similar to the ones in homemade chicken noodle soup.

NUTS
almonds pointy-ended with pitted brown shell enclosing a creamy white kernel that is covered by a brown skin.
cashews a rich, sweet, buttery nut; must be stored in the refrigerator because of its high fat content.
peanuts not, in fact, a nut, but the pod of a legume.
pine nuts also known as pignoli; not a nut, but a small, cream-coloured kernel from pine cones.
pistachios pale green, delicately flavoured nut inside hard off-white shells. They are crunchy with a delicately sweet taste.
To peel nuts, soak shelled nuts in boiling water for about 5 minutes; drain, then pat dry with absorbent paper. Rub skins with cloth to peel.
roasted roasting brings out the flavour of nuts. It can easily be done at home.

To roast nuts, place nuts in a single layer in dry pan and cook over a low heat until fragrant and just changed in colour; may also be roasted in a single layer in a pan in a moderate oven for eight to 10 minutes. Be careful to avoid burning nuts.

OIL
olive made from ripened olives.
peanut pressed from ground peanuts; most commonly used oil in Asian cooking because of its high smoke point (capacity to handle high heat without burning).
sesame made from roasted, crushed, white sesame seeds.
vegetable sourced from plants rather than animal fats.

OKRA
also known as bamia or lady fingers; a green, ridged, oblong pod with a furry skin used to thicken stews. Refrigerate fresh okra in a plastic bag for up to three days.

OMELETTE
An omelette consists of beaten egg cooked with butter or oil in a frying pan, often folded around a filling.
To prepare a thin omelette, brush heated wok with a little oil. Add egg; swirl to cover base of wok. Cook, uncovered, without stirring, about 3 minutes or until cooked through. Remove omelette from wok.

ONION
green also known as scallion or, incorrectly, shallot; an immature onion picked before the bulb has formed, having a long, bright-green edible stalk
red also known as red spanish, spanish or bermuda onion; a sweet-flavoured, large, purple-red onion.
shallots also called french shallots, golden shallots or eschalots; small, elongated, brown-skinned members of the onion family. Grows in tight clusters similar to garlic.
spring crisp, narrow green-leafed tops and a round sweet white bulb larger than green onions.
thai purple shallots also known as pink shallots or homm, are used throughout South-East Asia.

PANEER (see cheese).

PARSLEY FLAT-LEAF also known as continental or italian parsley.

PEKING DUCK PANCAKES a small, round crepe or pancake made with plain flour; they can be purchased commercially in Asian food stores.
To prepare pancakes, place in steamer set over large pan of simmering water. Steam about 5 minutes or until warm and pliable.

PITTA also known as lebanese bread. This wheat-flour pocket bread is sold in large, flat pieces that separate into two thin rounds. Also available in small thick pieces called *pocket pitta*.

POMEGRANATE MOLASSES (see page 39).

RICE
calrose a medium-grain rice that is extremely versatile; can substitute for short- or long-grain rices if necessary.
jasmine a long-grained, fragrant rice; white rice can be substituted, but the taste will not be the same.

ROTI a flatbread made from wheat flour and water, originating in India. Similar flatbreads are called chapati, phulka and parantha. Available from Asian food stores and supermarkets.

SAMBAL OELEK (also sambal ulek or olek); a salty paste made from ground chillies, garlic and vinegar.

SAKE japanese rice wine. If sake is unavailable, dry sherry, vermouth or brandy can be substituted.

SHALLOT (see onion).

SAUCES
black bean a chinese sauce made from fermented soy beans, spices, water and wheat flour.
char siu also known as chinese barbecue sauce. It is a paste-like ingredient that is dark-red-brown in colour and has sweet and spicy flavour. Made with fermented soy beans, honey and various spices.
chilli can come as a hot chinese variety, made of chillies, soy and vinegar; use sparingly, increasing the amount to suit your taste.
chilli bean made from fermented soy beans and chillies. This is a very hot sauce; use with discretion.

fish made from pulverised salted fermented fish (anchovies). Has a pungent smell and strong taste.
hoisin a rich, dark, sweet barbecue sauce made from soy beans, chillies, red beans and spices.
kecap asin a thick and salty dark soy sauce from Indonesia.
kecap manis a dark, thick sweet soy sauce. The soy's sweetness is derived from the addition of either molasses or palm sugar when brewed.
plum a thick, sweet and sour dipping sauce made from plums, vinegar, sugar, chillies and spices.
sweet chilli the comparatively mild, thai sauce made from red chillies, sugar, garlic and vinegar.
soy made from fermented soy beans.
tamari a thick, dark soy sauce made mainly from soy beans without the wheat used in standard soy sauce.
teriyaki a japanese sauce made with soy sauce, mirin and a little sugar.
oyster made from oysters and their brine, cooked with salt and soy sauce, and thickened with starches.
vegetarian mushroom oyster a dark sauce based on mushroom extract and soy beans that gives a flavour similar to oyster sauce.

SICHUAN PEPPERCORNS also known as szechuan or chinese pepper, native to the Sichuan province of China. A mildly hot spice having a distinctive peppery-lemon flavour and aroma.

SILVERSIDE also known as topside roast; used for making corned beef, usually sold vacuum-sealed in brine.

SOURDOUGH BREAD so-named, not because it's sour in taste, but because it's made by using a small amount of "starter dough", which contains a yeast culture mixed into flour and water. Part of the resulting dough is then saved to use as the starter dough next time.

SQUID a type of mollusc; also known as calamari. Buy squid hoods to make preparation easier.
To prepare, cut squid down centre to open out; score inside in a diagonal pattern then cut into thick strips.

STAR ANISE a dried star-shaped pod with an aniseed flavour.

SUGAR
brown a soft, fine sugar retaining molasses for it's colour and flavour. Substitute with dark brown sugar.
caster also known as superfine or finely granulated table sugar.
palm also known as nam tan pip, jaggery, jawa or gula melaka; made from the sap of the sugar palm tree. Light brown to black in colour and usually sold in rock-hard cakes; often grated before use. If unavailable substitute brown sugar.

TAMARIND CONCENTRATE (or paste) the distillation of tamarind juice into a condensed, compacted paste. Thick and purple-black, it requires no soaking or straining. Found in Asian supermarkets.

THAI BASIL also known as horapa; has small leaves, purplish stems and a slight licorice or aniseed taste.

TOFU also known as bean curd.
To prepare tofu, pat the tofu with absorbent paper then cut it into 2cm pieces. Spread tofu, in a single layer, on a tray lined with absorbent paper; cover with more absorbent paper then stand at least 10 minutes.

TORTILLA thin, round unleavened bread originating in Mexico; available in wheat or corn varieties.

TURMERIC also known as kamin, is a rhizome related to galangal and ginger, must be grated or pounded to release its somewhat acrid aroma and pungent flavour.

VIETNAMESE MINT a pungent and peppery narrow-leafed member of the buckwheat family.

WASABI an Asian horseradish, used in the pungent, green-coloured paste served with Japanese raw fish dishes; sold in paste or powdered form.

WOMBOK also known as chinese cabbage, peking cabbage, wong bok, or petsai. Elongated in shape with pale green crinkly leaves, it is the most common cabbage in South-East Asia.

ZUCCHINI also known as courgette.

CONVERSION CHART

MEASURES

One Australian metric measuring cup holds approximately 250ml; one Australian metric tablespoon holds 20ml; one Australian metric teaspoon holds 5ml.

The difference between one country's measuring cups and another's is within a two- or three-teaspoon variance, and will not affect your cooking results. North America, New Zealand and the United Kingdom use a 15ml tablespoon.

All cup and spoon measurements are level. The most accurate way of measuring dry ingredients is to weigh them. When measuring liquids, use a clear glass or plastic jug with the metric markings.

We use large eggs with an average weight of 60g.

DRY MEASURES

METRIC	IMPERIAL
15g	½oz
30g	1oz
60g	2oz
90g	3oz
125g	4oz (¼lb)
155g	5oz
185g	6oz
220g	7oz
250g	8oz (½lb)
280g	9oz
315g	10oz
345g	11oz
375g	12oz (¾lb)
410g	13oz
440g	14oz
470g	15oz
500g	16oz (1lb)
750g	24oz (1½lb)
1kg	32oz (2lb)

LIQUID MEASURES

METRIC	IMPERIAL
30ml	1 fluid oz
60ml	2 fluid oz
100ml	3 fluid oz
125ml	4 fluid oz
150ml	5 fluid oz (¼ pint/1 gill)
190ml	6 fluid oz
250ml	8 fluid oz
300ml	10 fluid oz (½ pint)
500ml	16 fluid oz
600ml	20 fluid oz (1 pint)
1000ml (1 litre)	1¾ pints

LENGTH MEASURES

METRIC	IMPERIAL
3mm	⅛in
6mm	¼in
1cm	½in
2cm	¾in
2.5cm	1in
5cm	2in
6cm	2½in
8cm	3in
10cm	4in
13cm	5in
15cm	6in
18cm	7in
20cm	8in
23cm	9in
25cm	10in
28cm	11in
30cm	12in (1ft)

OVEN TEMPERATURES

These oven temperatures are only a guide for conventional ovens. For fan-forced ovens, check the manufacturer's manual.

	°C (CELSIUS)	°F (FAHRENHEIT)	GAS MARK
Very slow	120	250	½
Slow	150	275-300	1-2
Moderately slow	160	325	3
Moderate	180	350-375	4-5
Moderately hot	200	400	6
Hot	220	425-450	7-8
Very hot	240	475	9

INDEX

ARE YOU MISSING SOME COOKBOOKS?

The Australian Women's Weekly Cookbooks are available from bookshops, cookshops, supermarkets and other stores all over the world. You can also buy direct from the publisher, using the order form below.

TITLE	RRP	QTY
100 Fast Fillets	£6.99	
A Taste of Chocolate	£6.99	
After Work Fast	£6.99	
Beginners Cooking Class	£6.99	
Beginners Simple Meals	£6.99	
Beginners Thai	£6.99	
Best Food Fast	£6.99	
Breads & Muffins	£6.99	
Brunches, Lunches & Treats	£6.99	
Cafe Classics	£6.99	
Cafe Favourites	£6.99	
Cakes Bakes & Desserts	£6.99	
Cakes Biscuits & Slices	£6.99	
Cakes Cooking Class	£6.99	
Caribbean Cooking	£6.99	
Casseroles	£6.99	
Casseroles & Slow-Cooked Classics	£6.99	
Cheap Eats	£6.99	
Cheesecakes: baked and chilled	£6.99	
Chicken	£6.99	
Chinese and the foods of Thailand, Vietnam, Malaysia & Japan	£6.99	
Chinese Cooking Class	£6.99	
Chocs & Treats	£6.99	
Cookies & Biscuits	£6.99	
Cooking Class Cake Decorating	£6.99	
Cupcakes & Fairycakes	£6.99	
Detox	£6.99	
Dinner Lamb	£6.99	
Dinner Seafood	£6.99	
Easy Comfort Food	£6.99	
Easy Curry	£6.99	
Easy Midweek Meals	£6.99	
Easy Spanish-Style	£6.99	
Food for Fit and Healthy Kids	£6.99	
Foods of the Mediterranean	£6.99	
Foods That Fight Back	£6.99	
Fresh Food Fast	£6.99	
Fresh Food for Babies & Toddlers	£6.99	
Good Food for Babies & Toddlers	£6.99	
Great Kids' Cakes (May 08)	£6.99	
Greek Cooking Class	£6.99	
Grills	£6.99	
Healthy Heart Cookbook	£6.99	
Indian Cooking Class	£6.99	
Japanese Cooking Class	£6.99	

TITLE	RRP	QTY
Just For One	£6.99	
Just For Two	£6.99	
Kids' Birthday Cakes	£6.99	
Kids Cooking	£6.99	
Kids' Cooking Step-by-Step	£6.99	
Low-carb, Low-fat	£6.99	
Low-fat Food for Life	£6.99	
Low-fat Meals in Minutes	£6.99	
Main Course Salads	£6.99	
Mexican	£6.99	
Middle Eastern Cooking Class	£6.99	
Midweek Meals in Minutes	£6.99	
Mince in Minutes	£6.99	
Mini Bakes	£6.99	
Moroccan & the Foods of North Africa	£6.99	
Muffins, Scones & Breads	£6.99	
New Casseroles	£6.99	
New Curries	£6.99	
New French Food	£6.99	
New Salads	£6.99	
One Pot	£6.99	
Party Food and Drink	£6.99	
Pasta Meals in Minutes	£6.99	
Quick & Simple Cooking	£6.99	
Rice & Risotto	£6.99	
Saucery	£6.99	
Sauces Salsas & Dressings	£6.99	
Sensational Stir-Fries	£6.99	
Simple Healthy Meals	£6.99	
Simple Starters Mains & Puds	£6.99	
Slim	£6.99	
Soup	£6.99	
Stir-fry	£6.99	
Superfoods for Exam Success	£6.99	
Tapas Mezze Antipasto & other bites	£6.99	
Thai Cooking Class	£6.99	
Traditional Italian	£6.99	
Vegetarian Meals in Minutes	£6.99	
Vegie Food	£6.99	
Wicked Sweet Indulgences	£6.99	
Wok Meals in Minutes	£6.99	
TOTAL COST	£	

Mr/Mrs/Ms _____

Address _____ Postcode _____

Day time phone _____ email* (optional) _____

I enclose my cheque/money order for £ _____

or please charge £ _____

to my: ☐ Access ☐ Mastercard ☐ Visa ☐ Diners Club

Card number | | | | | | | | | | | | | | | | | |

Expiry date _____ 3 digit security code *(found on reverse of card)* _____

Cardholder's name _____ Signature _____

To order: Mail or fax – photocopy or complete the order form above, and send your credit card details or cheque payable to: Australian Consolidated Press (UK), ACP Books, 10 Scirocco Close, Moulton Park Office Village, Northampton NN3 6AP. phone (+44) (0)1604 642200 fax (+44) (0)1604 642300 email books@acpuk.com or order online at www.acpuk.com
Non-UK residents: We accept the credit cards listed on the coupon, or cheques, drafts or International Money Orders payable in sterling and drawn on a UK bank. Credit card charges are at the exchange rate current at the time of payment. **Postage and packing UK:** Add £1.00 per order plus £1.75 per book. **Postage and packing overseas:** Add £2.00 per order plus £3.50 per book. All pricing current at time of going to press and subject to change/availability. **Offer ends 31.12.2009**
* By including your email address, you consent to receipt of any email regarding this magazine, and other emails which inform you of ACP's other publications, products, services and events, and to promote third party goods and services you may be interested in.

TEST KITCHEN

Food director Pamela Clark
Associate food editor Alexandra Somerville
Home economists Arianne Bradshaw, Lucy Bühler, Belinda Farlow, Nicole Jennings, Angela Muscat, Rebecca Squadrito, Kirrily Smith, Kellie-Marie Thomas

ACP BOOKS

General manager Christine Whiston
Editorial director Susan Tomnay
Creative director Hieu Chi Nguyen
Senior editor Wendy Bryant
Director of sales Brian Cearnes
Marketing manager Bridget Cody
Business analyst Rebecca Varela
Operations manager David Scotto
Production manager Victoria Jefferys
International rights enquires Laura Bamford
lbamford@acpuk.com

ACP Books are published by ACP Magazines a division of PBL Media Pty Limited
Group publisher, Women's lifestyle Pat Ingram
Director of sales, Women's lifestyle Lynette Phillips
Commercial manager, Women's lifestyle Seymour Cohen
Marketing director, Women's lifestyle Matthew Dominello
Public relations manager, Women's lifestyle Hannah Deveraux
Creative director, Events, Women's lifestyle Luke Bonnano
Research Director, Women's lifestyle Justin Stone
ACP Magazines, Chief Executive officer Scott Lorson
PBL Media, Chief Executive officer Ian Law

Produced by ACP Books, Sydney.
Published by ACP Books, a division of ACP Magazines Ltd, 54 Park St, Sydney; GPO Box 4088, Sydney, NSW 2001. phone (02) 9282 8618 fax (02) 9267 9438. acpbooks@acpmagazines.com.au www.acpbooks.com.au
Printed by Goodmanbaylis Ltd in the UK.

Australia Distributed by Network Services, phone +61 2 9282 8777 fax +61 2 9264 3278 networkweb@networkservicescompany.com.au
United Kingdom Distributed by Australian Consolidated Press (UK), phone (01604) 642 200 fax (01604) 642 300 books@acpuk.com
New Zealand Distributed by Netlink Distribution Company, phone (9) 366 9966 ask@ndc.co.nz
South Africa Distributed by PSD Promotions, phone (27 11) 392 6065/6/7 fax (27 11) 392 6079/80 orders@psdprom.co.za
Canada Distributed by Publishers Group Canada phone (800) 663 5714 fax (800) 565 3770 service@raincoast.com

A catalogue record for this book is available from the British Library.
ISBN 978-1-86396-485-2.
© ACP Magazines Ltd 2006
ABN 18 053 273 546
This publication is copyright. No part of it may be reproduced or transmitted in any form without the written permission of the publishers.
First published 2006. Reprinted 2007, 2008.

Scanpan cookware is used in the AWW Test Kitchen.
Send recipe enquiries to: askpamela@acpmagazines.com.au